THIS JOURNAL BELONGS TO

_____

Thera-pets Notebook

Notebook Pages Featuring 100 Colorable Encouraging Doodles from TheLatestKate

Kate Allan

mango
PUBLISHING
CORAL GABLES

Hello there,

Thank you very much for picking this notebook up! If you don't mind, I'd like to share some of my story with you.

Since I was very young, I've had a vicious mental critic that would berate me for every mistake. It often told me I was either "too much" or "not enough" for other people.

Luckily, I was able to visit a kind therapist in my mid-twenties who encouraged me to journal and argue with these unfair judgements. I then found that pairing kind words with cute animal drawings felt more "real" for me. I still had a hard time showing myself kindness, but I could feel comforted and encouraged by a furry friend.

Whether you use these pages to journal, take notes, make to-do lists, or write down ideas, I hope you find these friendly animals helpful too. And, if not, I hope you can at least feel a little less alone. There are many of us out here, quietly trying alongside you.

Cheering you on,
Kate Allan

stay soft

The world may be cold, but we don't have to be.

Today is a
brand new day,
and you are a
brand new you.

Good luck!

Here's a friendly reminder that the negative voice in your head is **not you**, and you are actually completely delightful

i know you feel anxious, but you forgot the part where YOU TOTALLY GOT THIS

There's no rule that says you have to have everything figured out RIGHT NOW.

Every step forward is progress.

Anxiety lies.

There is no doom incoming, and you're managing everything just fine.

Look at everything you have survived so far—

you weren't defeated then,

YOU WON'T BE DEFEATED NOW

Depression LIES.

There is no circumstance that is unchangeable.

There is no situation that is ever HOPELESS.

It's okay to be uncomfortable.

It's okay to be scared.

You will suceed in spite of these feelings.

Trying your best is all that matters.

The rest will fall into place.

you're not going to succeed at —everything— you try,

AND THAT'S OKAY

Feeling worried doesn't mean anything BAD is going to happen.

You're going to get through this fine; YOU ALWAYS FIND A WAY.

Whatever happens today, you will make it through.

With every challenge you meet, you gain **EXPERIENCE** — every day you're **LEVELING UP**

The truth is, you're
FAR MORE
CAPABLE
than you
feel.

The voice that tells you
that you aren't good enough
apparently
doesn't
know
you
AT
ALL.

YOU'RE
AMAZING.

It's okay to float along. It's okay to
JUST BE

you have survived
EVERY DAY
of your life so far

you really think
TODAY will be the one
that defeats you?

No beating yourself up anymore.

It doesn't help, and YOU DON'T DESERVE IT.

I rarely feel safe,
and I rarely feel capable,

**but I can
still do hard
things.**

If you're having a hard day that's because it IS a hard day. You are not bad at life.

you are
resilient,
you are
competent,
YOU WILL
HANDLE THIS

You belong in
the world today,
no matter
how "off" you
may feel.

Please try to be on your own side today.

Things change, and your efforts do matter. They will pay off in time.

you don't have to get it perfect; just showing up is enough

you are
enough
as you are
today

You don't have to always be advancing your life forward;

Some days you just gotta chill.

About the Author

Kate Allan is a bestselling author and illustrator from Washington State. She writes and draws about painful things but aims to make it okay with bright colors and sparkles. Under the handle The Latest Kate, she has a social media following of more than 400,000 people. Her work has been featured in *The Huffington Post, The Mighty, My Modern Met, Wear Your Voice Mag, The Patreon Blog, Sparklife,* and more.

Her work includes books, journals, coloring books, prints, and encouraging card decks, including *Thera-Pets, You Can Do All Things,* and *It's Your Weirdness that Makes You Wonderful.*

Copyright © 2022 by Kate Allan.
Published by Mango Publishing, a division of Mango Publishing Group, Inc.

Cover Design: Kate Allan
Cover Photo/illustration: Kate Allan
Layout & Design: Elina Diaz

Mango is an active supporter of authors' rights to free speech and artistic expression in their books. The purpose of copyright is to encourage authors to produce exceptional works that enrich our culture and our open society.

Uploading or distributing photos, scans or any content from this book without prior permission is theft of the author's intellectual property. Please honor the author's work as you would your own. Thank you in advance for respecting our author's rights.

For permission requests, please contact the publisher at:
Mango Publishing Group
2850 S Douglas Road, 4th Floor
Coral Gables, FL 33134 USA
info@mango.bz

For special orders, quantity sales, course adoptions and corporate sales, please email the publisher at sales@mango.bz. For trade and wholesale sales, please contact Ingram Publisher Services at customer.service@ingramcontent.com or +1.800.509.4887.

Therapets Notebook: Notebook Pages Featuring 100 Colorable Encouraging Doodles from TheLatestKate

ISBN: (print) 978-1-68481-213-4
BISAC category code ART017000, ART / Mixed Media

CPSIA information can be obtained
at www.ICGtesting.com
Printed in the USA
JSHW060314260523
42297JS00006B/7